For My Son, Nick

I wish I could go back in time, curl up with you and a book, and listen to your tiny voice recount your day. I cherish the sweet man you have become and hope you know how proud you make me every day.

my CHARACTER CHECK

a reflective resource for kids

(and adults)

concept and content

JEAN SMARTO

design

CODY WOOD

Pittsburgh, Pennsylvania
2025

Foreword

Intro

Check

Closing

Acknowledgments

Foreword

How can we spark deep conversations with children that teach them about good character?

I wrote this book to initiate meaningful conversations with our little ones about the importance of developing character and resilience. As a professional coach, I have learned the power of asking open-ended questions to encourage curiosity and invite exploration, feedback, and insights. These questions are key to establishing a daily practice of introspection, allowing us to learn from our experiences and become our best selves. The conversations we will have with our children will help them build confidence in their ability to solve problems, learn from mistakes, and understand that continuous learning should be an important goal in their lives.

The letters of the word "character" represent key virtues, reflected in poems and questions, that demonstrate our values to others. Fingers serve as memory devices to mark these virtues and remind us that our character is always in our own hands.

The reason I felt this book was so important to write lies in the research. Studies show a strong correlation between living by your values and your satisfaction in life. Living by your values has a positive effect, reduces internal conflicts, and leads to a more meaningful and fulfilling life. We are happier!

Although this is a children's book, I believe we can all benefit from gently reflecting on our daily conduct. The child we once were still lives inside us, regardless of our age.

Use your fingers to remember parts of your
"CHARACTER" as you go through your day.
Your thumb will be your final "CHECK"
when you think about what you learned today.

Dear Little One,

This book is written especially for you. Inside, you'll find poems about virtues that reflect your character. Your character is shaped by your daily actions and words. It's in your hands to build your character.

Stay curious and remember that every experience offers a lesson. Talk with the special people in your life; they want to help you learn and grow.

You'll have good days, great days, and challenging days that teach you to be better tomorrow.
And that's okay. Each new day is a fresh opportunity to become an even more amazing you!

Enjoy your journey!
- J

Choice

We all make choices every day,
it's how we learn and grow.

When you need to make a choice,
think of all the facts you know.

Trust your inner voice,
and let your true self show.

What kind of choices did you make today?

c

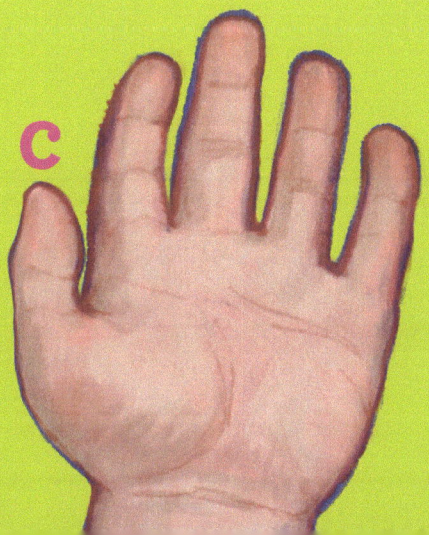

Honesty

It's your good heart inside
that tells you what to do.

Listen and do what's right
and say what's kind and true.

Let your actions always reflect
the very best version of you.

How does it feel when you are being honest?

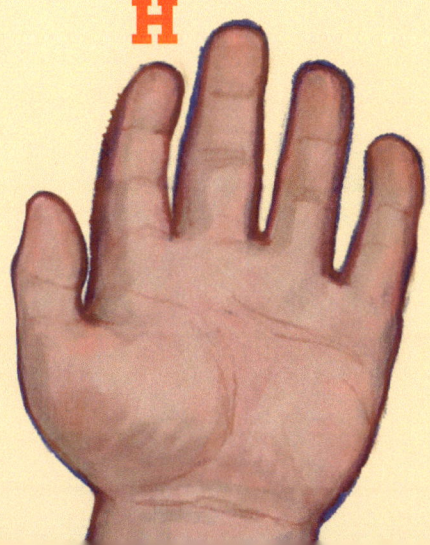

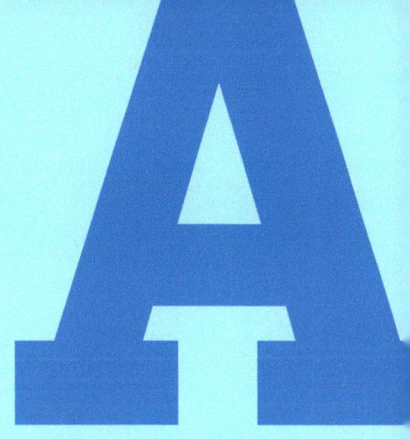

Attitude

Sometimes bad things happen
that make you feel sad or afraid.

The trick is to remember
strong emotions will soon fade.

Try to stay positive and calm
even when your nerves are frayed.

How did your attitude make a difference?

A

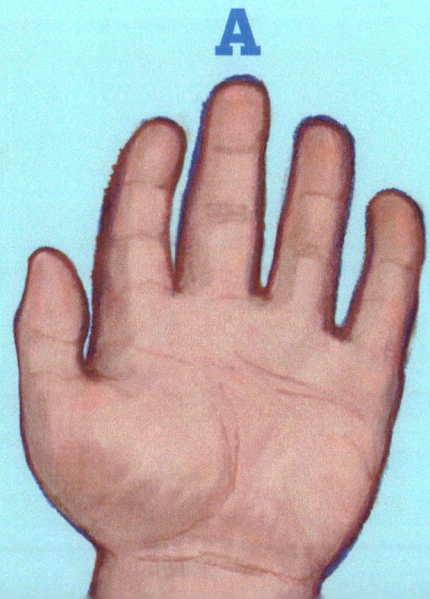

Responsibility

It is doing well all the tasks
that you're supposed to do.

Showing others that they can
always trust and depend on you.

Then proving you'll work hard
when alone or with your crew.

What are you responsible for at home or at school?

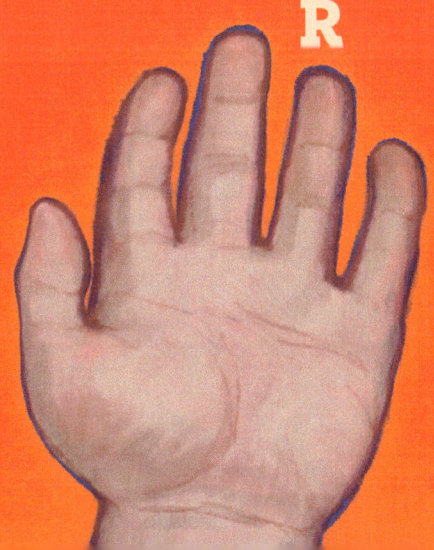

R

Appreciation

Thank others for kind words
and helping hands they share.

Tell them you are grateful
for how they show they care.

Enjoy being in the moment,
feeling thankful and aware.

How did you show your appreciation?

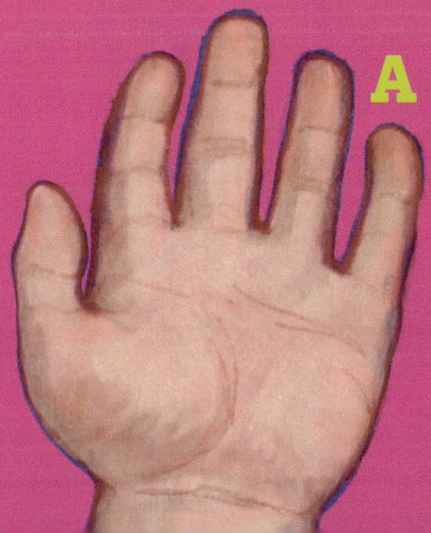

A

Courage

Be brave and try new things,
even if you have fears.

Take some risks and face
your big feelings and tears.

After, you will be proud,
and celebrate with cheers.

What was something new you tried today?

c

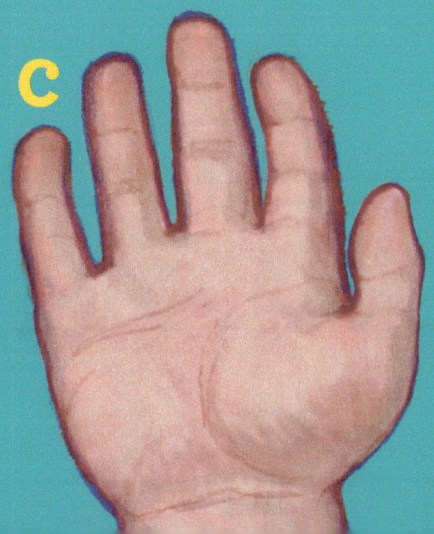

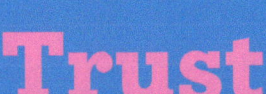

Trust

Trust is the foundation
for how our friendships start.

You rely on each other,
knowing both will do their part.

Friendships can be fragile,
stay true in your head and heart.

How was trust part of your day?

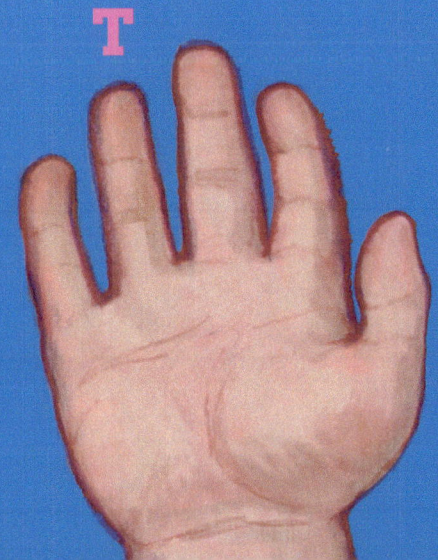

Empathy

It's trying to understand
what others feel inside.

We all have feelings
that we often try to hide.

Try to sense the emotions
of others by your side.

How did you let someone know you care?

E

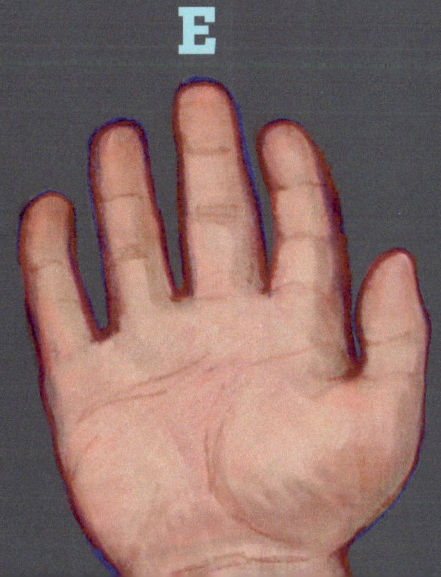

Respect

Respect is showing kindness
to yourself and others too.

Show you value their time
and belongings shared with you.

It's giving others your attention
even when it's hard to do.

How did you show respect?

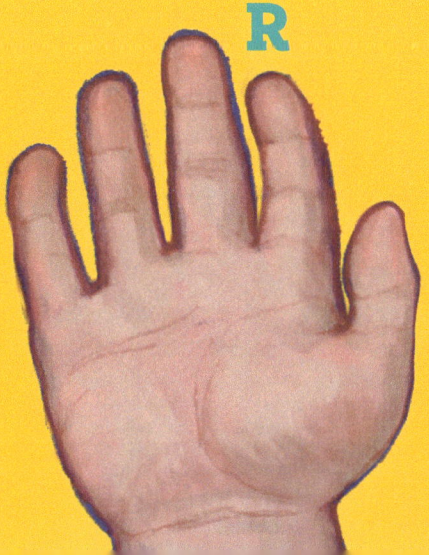

R

Check

Time to give your day a check.
Your thumb can go up or down.

Today may not be your best.
It's ok, no need to frown.

You get a new chance tomorrow.
Just learn, and turn it all around.

**Will you give yourself a thumbs up
or thumbs down for today?**

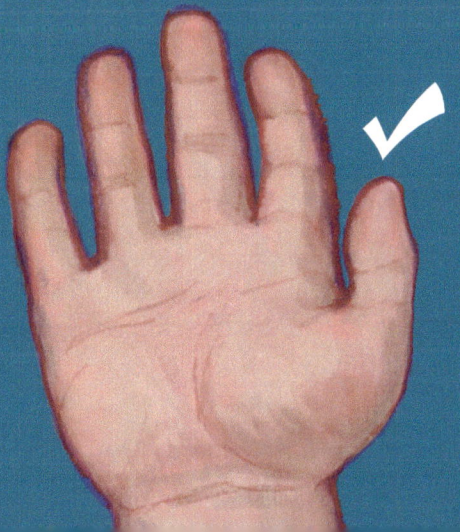

**What did you learn today
that you would like to
remember tomorrow?**

Acknowledgments

A special thanks to all the people who have helped me along the way. I have learned so many lessons from you. Your time and support have meant the world to me. I will forever be grateful for your presence in my life.

A heartfelt thanks to my illustrator, Cody, for your collaboration and creativity. Your illustrations brought this book together in a way words alone could never have achieved. Thank you for being part of this project and making it even more special!

Cody Wood is an animator, illustrator, designer, and painter. He has also spent time in student ministry and as a teacher.
"It's my firm belief that our most precious work is the relationships that we build with ourselves and others."

www.ingramcontent.com/pod-product-compliance
Lightning Source LLC
Chambersburg PA
CBHW040901120626
46551CB00001B/109